Inspirational Mind Food

Inspirational Mind Food

Positive Thoughts and Actionable Ideas
to Improve your Mind and Life

Christine M. Roberts

BOOKLOGIX®
Alpharetta, Georgia

ISBN: 978-1-61005-224-5

Library of Congress Control Number: 2012914954

Printed in the United States of America

♾This paper meets the requirements of ANSI/NISO Z39.48-1992 (Permanence of Paper)

Quotes taken from BrainyQuote.com, Motivational Today, and Motivating Quotes.

This book is dedicated to my wonderful husband who always encourages me to be the best I can be.

Every day is a fresh start and a new opportunity to create the life that we want and deserve. Have the courage to make changes today.
Decide to thrive...

Table of Contents

Introduction

I was ten years old sweeping the sidewalk at our broken down farm house. The memory is so vivid; I was wearing orange bell bottomed pants and a floral top (quite the fashionista!). I looked around at the dilapidated house, the junk cars in the pasture, my mom driving off to Bingo to escape, and my Dad as he took a case of beer to his workroom. I said to myself, "This is not going to be my life!"

Now, as a middle-aged woman with a wonderful life, I look back at that little girl and am amazed that she was so conscious of the circumstances and made a decision to redirect her future.

The first step to changing anything is being aware of what we're doing and/or thinking. That's what these short little life lessons are—moments when we can chose one way of thinking or acting in a positive way, or not. Sometimes you'll chose the positive and productive road and sometimes you won't, but unless you're thinking or paying attention to your thoughts, the situations will remain the same.

My belief is that regardless of where you came from or where you are today, you can accomplish just about anything that you set your mind to in order to reach your maximum potential. My hope is that by sharing these vignettes, the ideas within each story will ultimately add up to positive change for you.

You are special, deserving, and worthy of all the goodness life has to offer, but it's up to you to adjust and improve your path.

With Love, Prayers, and Kindness,

Christine

One | It's Not about Me, It's Not about You

I was driving on 400 North from Buckhead one day, and as I was approaching the toll booth, a car came riding up on my bumper tailgating me. My first thought was *What is this person's problem?* I found myself getting really ticked; it seemed like a deliberate case of harassment. Continuing down the highway I was getting more annoyed; as the traffic broke up, the car sped by me, got over to the right and off the ramp at the hospital exit.

Wow! I had a total paradigm shift. I thought to myself, *that person must have been going to the hospital.* I immediately felt embarrassed because, who am I? Why did I think it was about me? That person doesn't even know me and I was getting ticked off as if it was a personal offense.

Now this is not the only time this sort of thing happens, it can happen with people you know. Have you ever called a friend and they didn't return your call or you email someone and never hear back? Or you find out a couple of friends had lunch and you weren't invited? Or there's a hostess party that

1

someone committed to and didn't show up? You immediately start thinking, *I can't believe she didn't call or email me back/ didn't show up/ meet without inviting me!* Only to find out that your friend was on vacation, their email address had changed or is overwhelmed with some family crisis. The friends had lunch because they ran into each other at the store or maybe they had something specific to talk about? Or she didn't come to the party because money is tight and she didn't want to be embarrassed that she can't purchase something.

The bottom line is that 99.99 percent of the time, it's not about us. So the next time there's a situation where you start to question someone's actions and begin to take them personally...STOP and say "It's not about me." Odds are that person has "stuff" going on that has nothing to do with you.

Wouldn't it be great if we all gave the benefit of the doubt when these circumstances arise? It just might be a kinder, gentler world.

"The most important opinion you'll ever have is the one you hold of yourself."

- Denis Waitley

Stop worrying about what other people are thinking or doing and focus on being the best you can be.

Two| Striving For a Great Mind

I was invited to a party where I didn't know the people well.

While introducing myself and meeting everyone, I heard the beginning of an interesting discussion. The conversation went abruptly from ordinary small talk to personal; "friends" not present were being discussed. Nothing horrible was said, but a lot of the comments weren't very complimentary either. Okay, let's call it by its name; this was a gossip fest.

Then, to my own horror, even though I did not know the persons of interest, I was tempted to add my two cents so I could fit in.

This prompted me to ask myself a few questions. You know that internal dialog that we all have?

- First, is this right? Should this conversation be taking place?
- If I weren't here, what would be said about me?

- How can I change the subject?

This experience left me with an uneasy feeling. Have you ever found yourself in this situation? Or are you the one initiating the comments? We all have been guilty of gossiping at some level and sometimes it's like a drug and we just can't stop ourselves!

There's a quote by Eleanor Roosevelt that sticks in my mind whenever this temptation comes over me: "Great minds talk about ideas. Average minds talk about events. Small minds talk about people."

I don't know about you, but striving for a great mind or at least an average mind is where I want to be. As enticing as it is to gossip, and at that moment seems fulfilling, at the end of the day we never really feel good about it. So when that gossip drug starts sucking you in just listen to that little voice inside your head saying, "Strive for a great mind, strive for a great mind..."

Just think how much better the world, or at least our communities, would be if we focused our energy on IDEAS.

"Govern thy life and thoughts as if the whole world were to see the one, and read the other."

- Thomas Fuller

When the urge to gossip creeps in STOP yourself and as many of our Mom's would say

"If you don't have something good to say, don't say anything at all."

Three | Promises –
The Key to How We
Feel About Ourselves

The most important promises we make are the promises we make to ourselves. How many of us have said to ourselves, "I'm going to the gym every day for the next month," or "I'm going to lose 20 lbs. in 2 weeks." Many of us are great at making lists, but at the end of the day see only one or two items checked off. What does that feel like to make that promise and then not keep it.....terrible right?

Many of us minimize how important those promises are because we think since we made the promise privately, nobody will ever know. In fact, we should be honoring ourselves as the most important person.

We must be sure that we are striking balance in our lives; if you live with the idea that Balance is the Key to life and strive to achieve that, and then you are much more likely to realize that balance. Too much of anything isn't good, having a big bowl of ice cream...good, five big bowls ...not good. That sure sounds easier said than done... huh? But again striving to be better every day is what it's all about, we're all a work in progress and it's important to be kind to ourselves and only compare ourselves to ourselves.

Confidence, self-assurance, and happiness can only come from within so let's focus our energy on being the best we can be and all the other relationships in our lives will improve. Make those realistic promises and keep them because at the end of the day we have to be true to ourselves.

"Act as if what you do makes a difference. It does."

- William James

Write it Down!

Write down three promises to yourself and keep them.

Four | Good Day, Bad Day –
It's All About Attitude

My husband and children went on their annual camping trip. Bonding time for them, nirvana for me! A clean house and free time to do projects that are always put on the back burner...like putting together our family photo album, organizing closets; finishing decorating projects, etc...you know what I am talking about.

The minute they left I headed to my favorite store. Browsing around with no time constraints gave me such a feeling of joy, that is, until I needed some assistance. My shopping high came to a screeching halt when the employee I asked for help gave me the annoyed, you're bugging me look. She then said "What do ya need?" I think she would have preferred to say "You're a pain in the neck and I really don't want to help you!"

Wow! How could I go from feeling so good to feeling so bad? My internal dialogue was not pretty, but we're all taught to give the benefit of the doubt; so I told myself that this young lady must be having a bad day. When I asked her if that was the case she sweetened up quite a bit.

13

Has this ever happened to you? Maybe you're on vacation, taking the children out for ice cream, or just heading to the grocery store. Life seems pretty good until you come across that person with the bad attitude and it takes all we've got not to let it affect us.

Luckily there's the opposite side. How about the times when we encounter someone who is energetic and uplifting and their positive attitude brightens our day. Wouldn't we all like to be that person?

There is quote from Zig Ziglar that says, "Your attitude not your aptitude that determines your altitude." I had a Boss once tell me that he would rather hire the person who has the best attitude as opposed to the smartest, because he can teach a person what they need to know.

Regardless of what is going on, everyone prefers to be around the positive person. So the next time we're having a bad day or run into a person who is having a bad day, let's just ask ourselves, *How do we want to feel or how do we want to make someone else feel?* And decide to choose the positive attitude, how great would that be? Good day, bad day, it's all up to us!

"It's not what happens to you that determines how far you will go in life; it is how you handle what happens to you."

- Zig Ziglar

The next time someone else is having a bad day, <u>make the decision</u> that it will not affect your day. Take the opportunity to positively affect someone's day and initiate at least one act of random kindness.

Five| Just Ask...Why Not? What's the Worst that Can Happen?

How many times did you want to ask for something, but you just let it go?

Whether it's asking to have your burger cooked longer, a different hotel room, an appointment with a potential employer, coffee with someone who is in an industry you're interested in, asking for the job that you're interviewing for, or even deeper than that, asking for forgiveness for something you have done—but you just do not ask.

Why is that? Fear, right? Fear of what?

Here is what I always say to myself when I want to ask for something, but I am afraid: *What is the worst that can happen?*

I then visualize all the bad things that can happen, list them out, and examine them closely.

Bad Scenarios:

- You die. Now that is not going to happen—well I guess it depends on the situation, but odds are pretty low.
- You are humiliated. Okay that would stink, but really at the end of the day, it's not that bad—and you did not die.
- The person tells you you're an idiot. Again, odds are pretty low.
- Your request is answered with, "No!" Well again, that would be the pits, but you had a 50/50 shot and they might say "Yes!" So, at least half the time, you will get the answer you are looking for.

Now if you are a person of faith, here is a really compelling reason to ask...It is in the Bible! "Ask and it will be given to you" (Matt 7:7). Now you cannot argue with that!

The bottom line is that nothing happens unless we take action, so go for it! When that little voice in your head says, *Ah, forget it!* Just give it a whack and ask yourself, *why not?* After all, what is the worst that can happen?

Do this and you will be amazed at all the good stuff that will happen in your life.

"Never be bullied into silence. Never allow yourself to be made a victim. Accept no one's definition of your life; define yourself."

- Harvey Fierstein

Write it Down!

What are three things you've wanted to ask for? Write them down. Make them happen.

Six| Life is what We Make it – No Excuses!

Several years ago, I found myself in a place where I was unhappy in my life. I had taken a promotion and moved to another state, but quickly discovered the job was a nightmare! My boss was unrealistically demanding and the job required me to travel 90 percent of the time. I was single and because of the travel, I had no time to make friends. My quality of life was terrible!

It dawned on me one day that I had been having the same gripes and conversations for months; every time I spoke with someone, it was the same story and complaints. Frankly, I was sick of listening to myself, let alone anyone else having to listen to me. So I made the decision to change my situation. I took action. I found a new job that I loved making great money, moved back to Atlanta, met my husband, and before I knew it, my life was back on track.

Do you know anyone who complains about the same things every time you speak with them? Their marriage stinks, the kids don't listen, they hate their job, they don't have any friends, there's nothing to do, they're stressed out with all the activities every weekend, and on and on. Or is this you?

Well, why not change your situation? Find ways to enhance your marriage, attend parenting classes, participate in networking groups, get involved with your church, make an effort to meet people with your same interest, do an internet search for things to do in your town, and finally, STOP filling your weekend with so many events.

While most of us know solutions to our problems, actually doing something about them is another thing entirely. All too often we would rather complain about things before we put in the effort to make changes. So many times we feel like we're stuck in a situation but we're not! As we know, the only two things in life that are certain are death and taxes. Other than that we are so blessed to live in the United States of America where we have the freedom to create the life we want to live.

If life isn't what you want it to be, assess the situation, and then empower yourself and make changes...Life is what we choose to make it! When you take charge of your life and embrace positive changes, you become a role model to your children and others for how to live life to its fullest. Now have the courage to make it happen. You can do it!

"The best way to get started is to stop talking and begin doing."

- Walt Disney

Write it Down!

Write down five things you want to accomplish then reverse engineer how you can achieve them.

Seven | We Can Only "Fix" Ourselves

Back in my single days I found myself in relationships where I was constantly having conversations with friends like...*He needs to change; He just needs to be more expressive, be more affectionate; Listen better; Be more responsible*...and on and on. Everything was about how the other person needed to improve. Then one day I realized that the only person I could change was me; all the effort I was expending was futile. When I started putting energy into "fixing" me instead of other people, life got a lot more enjoyable—and amazingly healthy relationships started "coincidentally" showing up in my life.

Now, the idea of fixing or changing someone not only applies to romantic relationships, but also applies in any other relationship. There are times when we feel frustrated about how our children, mother, father, in-laws, or some friends act. And we are constantly pointing the finger at them discussing or thinking how things would be so much better if they were different. That's when it's time to turn the finger in the opposite direction and ask ourselves, how can we be different?

The definition of insanity is doing the same thing over and over again and expecting different results. So start asking yourself, *Why am I the way I am?* Immerse yourself in taking care of *you* to be the best that *you* can be. Read self-help books, seek counseling, participate in some seminars or retreats, and/or join a small group with church. Wayne Dyer, a self-help guru, says "When you change the way you look at things, the things you look at change." It takes a lot of courage to address our own issues but it is so worth it!

We're all a work in progress so we're never finished growing and improving. When we take charge of ourselves, it is an amazing, empowering feeling. It may surprise you how all those others that we used to try to fix suddenly have changed. What if we all could have peace with who we are? How much better our world and relationships would be.

"Everything that is past is either a learning experience to grow on, a beautiful memory to reflect on, or a motivating factor to act upon."

- Denis Waitley

Identify the top issue in your life and take action today to fix it.

Eight| Positive Talk –
The Words We Say
Make a Difference

When our son was a baby, we were trying to teach him how to eat, where he could go in the house, what he could touch. You know that age when they're into everything and you can never relax! We said things like:

- Don't throw your food on the floor
- Don't go up those stairs
- Don't touch that vase

Guess what he did...threw his food...went up the stairs...and touched the vase! After seeing that this was not working, we realized that everything we said focused on what he couldn't do, instead of speaking positively and telling him what we wanted him TO do:

- Keep your food on your tray
- Stay in the living room
- Keep your hands to down

It was amazing the results that we got when we remembered to do this. But don't get me wrong, we still couldn't relax.

Does this ever happen to you? We all speak this way to a certain extent; to our significant others, children, parents, coworkers, and we don't even realize it. *You never help me; don't run in the house; you can't do it that way.* As opposed to: *I appreciate you taking out the garbage; please walk when you are in the house; and here is how you do it.*

Those we speak to using the negative verbiage usually don't realize it at a conscious level either; they just respond by tuning us out or getting angry...but hey, who can blame them? And we have all had someone speak to us that way as well, and we often have the same reactions.

When you notice that negative terminology entering your mind or slipping off your tongue with others or even with yourself, stop and think or say the opposite. Try it. Hopefully, it'll become more of a habit. It's not easy to change how we speak or think, and usually our comments are reactive but at least it's worth a shot. What the heck? It's those subtle changes that we strive to make that ultimately add up and improve our life, even if it's just a little.

Just think if we all changed our language to speak positively and focus our words on what we want. How much better off we'd be.

"The most important single ingredient in the formula of success is knowing how to get along with people."

– Theodore Roosevelt

For the next twenty-one days, pay attention to what you say and how you say it. Change the negative to positive.

Nine| Focus on Appreciation

My husband and I went on a getaway weekend where a childhood friend of his is a manager at a five-star resort (we're hanging with the right people). It was an amazing weekend with gourmet meals, spa day, and golf. The friend had organized the entire event and created some incredible memories. One thing I noticed while on the trip was that regardless of all the terrific things he had arranged, his wife seemed to constantly have some type of criticism.

"Why isn't there any jam for the biscuits? "How come you bought spread instead of butter?" etc. The look on his face would reveal subtle hurt but he would then crack a joke and she'd respond by saying "Oh, I'm just teasing."

These comments made me think about my own conversations with people, especially my husband. As much as I hoped that I don't do that, if I'm really honest with myself I have to confess that I do make those types of comments now and again...actually more than I'd like to admit.

Do you make critical remarks to someone in your life? Why do we do that? Maybe we think we're being funny, but being funny shouldn't be at someone else's expense. Have you ever had a person do that to you? It is hurtful when we feel like we've made a lot of effort putting something together only to have another person come along and point out the "one" thing we missed.

How about when our husband's go to the store and get everything on our list, but got white grape juice instead of apple and we say, "Ughhh, don't you read the labels?" instead of saying, "Thank you." Or our children bring home their report card with mostly A's except for one B or C and we focus on why they didn't get all A's, instead of praising them for what a great job they did getting all those excellent grades.

When these scenarios take place and the critical words are on the tip of our tongues, maybe if we take a moment and think of the word "appreciate," that'll stop us and we can rephrase our response. There's a fine line between teaching someone and defeating someone. What if we make the decision that if there is some sort of criticism, we counter it with twice as many positive comments? Again, back to treat others the way we want to be treated. It is a simple saying but hard to implement sometimes; although it sure would be nice. I bet our families would love it too.

"Your mental attitude is something you can control outright and you must use self-discipline until you create a positive mental attitude – your mental attitude attracts to you everything that makes you what you are."

- Napoleon Hill

Start today and tell those you love how awesome they are; only focusing on all the goodness they possess.

Ten| Having Peace

I just returned from a three-day retreat where the pain of being molested as a child was finally put behind me. This burden had been with me my entire life and although it had affected me over the years it was easier to brush it aside and pretend that it was in the past. Although, when my daughter turned five, the same age that I was when the molestation happened, the pain and hurt resurfaced. As hard as it was to face the pain, it was so worth it! Forgiving the person who had done this to me, as well as forgiving myself for thinking it was somehow my fault, was amazing! The best word to describe that feeling is *peace.*

Is there some pain from your past that haunts you but it's just too scary to face? Maybe there was alcoholism, emotional or physical abuse, neglect, or bullying. It doesn't have to be that dramatic, maybe the adults in your life worked a lot and you didn't feel important?

Most of us have something that haunts us from the past and whether we realize it or not, these things do affect our lives in some way.

If you have that "twinge" when you think about a memory or an event, then it probably will do your soul and spirit some good to look at it. Have the courage to reach out and face it. There are seminars, retreats, counselors, books, support groups, as well as other resources you can find.

We're all a work in progress, and as difficult as it can be to face the demons of our past, seeking to forgive those who have hurt us, as well as forgive ourselves, is so powerful. Forgiveness is a concept that can be so difficult to grasp, but it's a choice that we make for us. It doesn't mean that what happened is okay, it just means that we won't carry the burden on ourselves anymore.

How great would life be if we all faced those unresolved hurts? Having peace, now that's a great way to live!

"Live every day like it's your last cause one day you're gonna be right."

- Ray Charles

Write it Down!

Who do you have to forgive?
Have courage and forgive today!

Eleven| Gratitude—the Root of Happiness

I had taken time off from my career that I loved to care for our children full-time which I am thankful for, but frankly it was tough. Our disposable income had decreased dramatically. Okay, it was nonexistent! My husband traveled frequently and because we don't have family in town, I felt totally stressed out and trapped. Being home with a baby and toddler was so much harder than anything I had ever done. I envied the moms who were home full-time and loving it.

If anyone could have read my thoughts they would have been mortified. I had turned into this negative thinking person and it was awful! I remember saying to myself *this is not me!* How could I have gone from a happy-go-lucky, joyful person to this unappreciative miserable person? One day it hit me. I realized the main thing I was missing was gratitude.

Do you ever feel this way? Life can seem so difficult with all the demands of running the house, managing schedules, thinking the house isn't big enough, or the car isn't good enough, the children don't listen, our spouse doesn't help enough, paying the bills with sometimes, not enough money...whatever you perceive to be lacking in your life. And we find ourselves constantly focused on what we *don't have.*

For me, I had to get the pendulum swinging the opposite way from predominate negative thoughts to predominate positive thoughts. As cheesy as it sounds, I started listening to motivational CD's, turned off the news as well as other negative programming, started journaling everything that I'm grateful for, listened to inspirational music, and tried to "feed" my mind and spirit only positive, good "stuff."

There's no quick fix, everything in life is baby steps but it's a matter of stepping in the direction that you want your life to go...deciding what life we want to live and being purposeful to head that way. If we get down to the "root" and seek out gratitude then the chances of being happy and fulfilled will increase dramatically. What do you think?

"Happiness doesn't depend on what we have, but it does depend on how we feel toward what we have. We can be happy with little and miserable with much."

- William Dempster Hoard

 **Write it Down!**

Write down all the things you are grateful for starting with the fact that you are breathing right now, your eyes allow you to read and your brain allows you to think.

Twelve| We're All Scared; Just Say "Hi"

I went to a conference where I didn't know anyone. Even though I consider myself outgoing and relatively self-assured, there were still butterflies in my stomach. The thought of walking in and having to meet new people and make conversation was terrifying. As I stood and looked around, I noticed others standing around alone as well—probably with the same apprehension that I felt. As I contemplated what to do, the stress was building. Finally I sucked it up and mustered up the courage to walk over to a lady standing by herself and said, "Hi, my name is Christine, what's your name?" With that the tension subsided and I made a friend.

Have you ever felt that same fear? Maybe it's going to a neighborhood party, a networking function for work, attending a new church, a PTA meeting, going to the local pool, whatever it may be, where there are people you don't know.

How do you handle those situations? It can definitely be nerve-racking and scary, but guess what? Everyone is scared. If we realize that and focus on helping the other people not feel scared by just introducing ourselves, it's amazing how easy it is to meet people.

The other awkward thing that can happen is we see someone we don't know well but have met and don't remember their name so instead of "fessing" up to that, we totally ignore or avoid them. Rather than do that how about we just say something like, "I know we have met before, please remind me of your name. My name is..." Let's face it they probably forgot our name too so by coming clean it takes the pressure off all of us.

This is not only a great lesson for us adults but also a lesson for our children. Just knowing that we're all nervous and scared in situations where we don't know anyone, all we need to do is say, "Hi. What's your name? My name is..." Not only will we learn how to relax and embrace the experience but we'll also make a lot of friends.

How great would that be if everyone just introduced themselves, and then there wouldn't be any reason to be scared.

"Fear makes strangers of people who would be friends."

- Shirley MacLaine

At the next social event go up and introduce yourself to at least five people.

Thirteen| "Complete the Task" for a Great Day!

It was nine p.m. and as I sat looking at my "to do" list, frustration and disappointment set in. How can I be so busy ALL DAY and then feel like I've accomplished nothing? I find myself constantly going from one thing to the next but never finishing what was started. It's like being a mouse on a wheel more often than not.

Do you ever feel that way? It seems that every day more things pile up and come along to distract us! The laundry needs to be folded and put away, there's no milk, its teacher appreciation week, the car needs new brakes, there's birthday presents that need to be purchased by Saturday and on and on. With family members needing something, instant messaging, texting, email, face book, twitter, etc. there's almost no way to stay focused. But I mean, hey we've got to be connected, right?

The only times I've had success crossing items off my list is when I force myself to take one task at a time and complete it. It takes so much self-control and discipline. So of course it doesn't happen all the time, but I literally have that internal voice continually saying "complete the task, complete the task." If anyone could read my mind they would surely think that I'm a bit strange. But when I keep this dialogue going and actually "complete the task" there is such a feeling of accomplishment and at the end of the day this is priceless. Give it a try.

Even if we can't finish all that we've set out to do each day, just crossing a few things off our list will make it a great day! Remember, have that little voice saying "complete the task, complete the task..."

"The ability to concentrate and to use your time well is everything if you want to succeed in business—or almost anywhere else for that matter."

- Lee Iacocca

Write it Down!

For every task that you start today force yourself to complete it before going on to the next task, do this for the next seven days.

Fourteen| Let's Keep Our Two Cents

I was talking with a friend the other day who went through a difficult divorce a couple of years ago. After being dedicated to raising the children and running the home for the past ten years, she was thrust into having to find employment outside the home, generate enough money to make ends meet, figure out how to manage a not so cooperative ex-husband, as well as entering back into the dating scene. The various challenges she has had to face and is still facing are exponential. When I saw her, it was obvious that her spirit was broken. When I asked how she was doing she shared with me some of the pain she was going through. As I listened I couldn't help but add my two cents offering advice about what she could or should do.

In the middle of the conversation another friend stopped by and our conversation was interrupted. We never finished the discussion and ended up parting ways. While heading home there was an uneasy feeling in my gut. I realized that my friend never asked for my advice! When we left each other I'm sure she didn't feel any better after talking to me, in fact, she probably felt worse. I apologized the next time I saw her but at that point it was probably too late.

Have you ever done this? Or has someone done this to you? Maybe there are relationship issues with a significant other, financial challenges, behavioral issues with children, work related or other family "stuff," whatever it may be. There are always going to be obstacles in our lives at one point or another.

When we are going through difficult times, we just want someone to listen and offer words of encouragement. It seems that other's situations are always much clearer to us than our own, but at the end of the day each of us has to figure things out for ourselves. We all want to be heard and validated when facing a lot of pain; kindness is all that we're looking for. As hard as it can be to just listen, it definitely is the most appreciated action.

So unless someone specifically asks, let's keep our two cents to ourselves and hopefully others will do the same.

"The most powerful and predictable people-builders are praise and encouragement."

- Brian Tracy

Provide the next person who shares their concerns/anxiety/ frustration only encouraging words and leave it at that.

Fifteen| Positive Energy vs. Complaining – Which Sounds Good to You?

I was returning home from a business trip in Chicago in a great mood ready to get back to my family. It was the normal routine. I walked off the rental car bus, went to the Delta kiosk, picked up my boarding pass, but then boom there it was—an unbelievably long line to get through security. I'm used to the Atlanta airport where there are a lot of people but at least the line moves quickly. Now here I am at O'Hare and it is gridlock. Not only is the line long but it isn't moving! The dialogue in my head was ugly: "What the $&#@& is going on here? Why isn't this line moving? This is ridiculous!" The temptation to start complaining to those around me was almost unbearable! But I said to myself, *Don't do it, don't complain, it won't change anything.* So instead I asked the guys in front of me about the logos on their luggage and we struck up a conversation, ultimately laughing about the security log jam. Then suddenly the line started moving.

Now that is one circumstance where self-discipline actually stuck, but if we think about how we react in these types of frustrating scenarios, we might be surprised at how often we go down the unconstructive path of griping. And we have all been in the situation when someone else gets all worked up, and then we get on the bandwagon of getting all worked up as well. That's never enjoyable.

It makes sense to voice concern when it is a circumstance that can possibly be changed. Although with some things like planes being delayed, only one security line, restaurants not having the item we want, or other things beyond our control, we just have to deal with it. Heading down a negative road doesn't get us anywhere except in a bad mood.

Something you may want to try is pretending you are on one of those reality shows where there is a hidden camera. How would you want to be portrayed if your actions or reactions were being captured for all to see? This usually keeps me on my toes. Or try to find something else to talk about with those around you. This typically lightens the mood and the time goes faster. You may even make a new friend.

It's easy to head in the direction of complaining in difficult situations but when we start considering that option, what if we all chose positive energy instead? How great would that be?

"Happiness depends more on the inward disposition of mind than the outward circumstances."

- Benjamin Franklin

As hard as it will be the next time you're in a situation that tempts you to complain, <u>make the decision</u> not to.

Sixteen| Be Self-Assured...
Others Aren't Concerned

I just returned from the OYou! (Oprah) conference at the World Congress Center which I attended by myself. While standing in the atrium observing all the activity, it seemed as if hundreds of people were passing by and a comfortable self-assured sensation came over me...there are some benefits to getting older. It was fun and interesting just observing people and enjoying all of the learning opportunities available.

While contemplating all that was going on, my thoughts drifted back to the first time I went out in public alone. I was at a restaurant at the mall on a break from that first job. At a ripe old age of seventeen, the insecurity was almost unbearable. Everyone in the diner was definitely staring at me wondering why I was there eating by myself...I was just sure of that.

Have you ever felt this way, or do you still? Maybe there's a class you want to take, a restaurant you want to try, a movie you are interested in seeing, or some other event that you eagerly want to attend but none of your friends or family can or want to go.

61

So often we stay home because of the concern about what people will think. We must be total goobers to be out by ourselves! Another aspect is that we are paranoid that people are talking about us. What I've discovered is that others really don't care what we are doing.

That may sound harsh but it's true. If there is something you want to do, *go for it* even if no one else wants to take part. When you do take that step, and insecure emotions start to show themselves, just say to yourself, *why do I think others care what I'm doing?* That question is quite humbling and works for me every time.

What if we did our best to take charge of what makes us joyful or at least seek out some new adventures even if we have to go it alone? Maybe life could be a bit more fulfilling? Let's be self-assured and stop worrying about what other people think and do some of the things that make us happy. Others really aren't concerned anyway.

"Learn as if you were going to live forever. Live as if you were going to die tomorrow."

- Mahatma Gandhi

Write it Down!

Identify two events or activities that you want to do and sign up then let whomever you want to invite know about it, hopefully they'll come but, if not, you've got your plan. Way to go!

Seventeen| Concerned About Being "Judged"? Maybe there's a Good Reason

There was a time in my life when I was making poor decisions, like spending time with people that I shouldn't and spending money that I didn't have. I wasn't sharing these activities with anyone because I decided it wasn't any of their business and I didn't want to be judged!

Do you have any circumstances in your life where you feel this way? Maybe you're spending time with a "friend" but your significant other or close friends wouldn't understand or you couldn't help but buy that $5,000 plasma television even though your credit cards are maxed out and you owe friends or family money. Maybe your doctor has told you that if you don't take better care of yourself that your life is in jeopardy, but you keep that information to yourself as you continue to consume those Bud Lights and country cooking. But, "Hey it's nobody's business!"

Well if we are doing the "right" thing and being responsible then our conscience will be clear and there isn't energy spent on worry about being judged, right? Sometimes we can convince ourselves that what we are doing is okay; we can rationalize just about anything, can't we? The benchmark for knowing if that rationalization is adequate is if we want to keep it to ourselves. That always works for me; if I hesitate about telling someone then I shouldn't do it, as simple as that.

So if you are feeling like "its" no one's business then maybe it's a good opportunity to take inventory and say to yourself: *if I'm concerned about being judged, maybe there's a good reason.* Think about it.

We all know what is right and what is wrong, so stop trying to kid yourself or others; having a clear conscience is the way to live. What if we all decided to live life making the "right" choices? Now that's a resolution worth sticking to year round!

"Character is higher than intellect. A great soul will be strong to live, as well as strong to think."

- Ralph Waldo Emerson

What are you keeping a secret?
Confess or stop doing it!

Eighteen| Positive Thinking – A Form of Denial?

A beautiful woman sat down next to me while I gazed out at the Pacific Ocean pondering my life. We struck up a conversation sharing our stories. When she asked me about mine, I explained that my move to California was considered a prestigious promotion. I managed the company's largest customer for the country, the position required 95 percent travel, all escalation issues funneled to me, sixty to seventy (plus) hour work weeks, and "challenges" at every turn. But I told her that I was doing my best to focus on the positive. I was listening to every motivational CD ever made, it seemed, and trying to have a paradigm shift about how I viewed things.

The following words changed my life...She said, "I think positive thinking can be a form of denial, if you hate it, hate it! Why are you trying to make it something it's not?"

It was as if the sky parted and angels began to sing. Yes, she was right! The job was a nightmare! At that moment I began the process of changing my situation.

Are there people or situations that you are trying to convince yourself are good and positive? Is there a relationship, either romantic or platonic, that just doesn't work or takes so much energy, but you keep trying to convince yourself that it's not so bad? It may be a job that you think you are stuck doing, maybe your son's sports team experience is running you ragged and it turns out he doesn't even like it that much. It could be that playgroup while, theoretically, sounds good but you don't have anything in common with the other mom's.

Being positive and optimistic is terrific, but there may be times when we are spending a lot of energy convincing ourselves that something is good when it's not. If that's the case then we have to stop trying to fit a square peg into a round hole. Whatever it is either make it right or move on...it's okay!

What if we all took charge of those situations that don't bring us joy, wouldn't that be a great life? Positive thinking or a form of denial...hmmm which one is it?

"Never fear shadows. They simply mean that there's a light somewhere nearby."

- Ruth E. Renkei

Write it Down!

Think about and write down at least two things that you are doing that aren't working and stop doing them.

Nineteen| Just Go, It'll Be Fun!

It's five o'clock the Friday before Memorial Day weekend and the last day of school. I'm sitting at my desk having just finished a report that I must to present to Executive Management next week. My brain is fried as I've scrambled to complete it on top of all the other responsibilities as mom, wife, mentor, room mom, writer...oh gosh, like everyone else the list goes on, I don't want to think about it. Right now all I want to do is enter a vegetative state while I lie on the couch and watch HGTV.

But there's a pool party in the neighborhood and our children are now begging me to go...ughhhh that is the last thing I want to do! My husband being the smart guy that he is says, "Honey I'll take them, you stay home and relax." What an awesome man! But after they left the twinge of guilt set in and I said to myself. *Just go. It'll be fun.* I really didn't feel that way but figured if I said that enough than maybe I'd convince myself.

So off I went to the party, it was like something out of a movie with Dad's in belly flop contests, and the neighborhood coach as DJ with hysterical commentary, the only thing missing was a Babe Ruth bar in the pool. I had a blast!

Does this ever happen to you? There's a party or event and it's much easier for us to stay home never leaving our comfort zone. Maybe there are friends that you'd love to meet up with, an event to attend or activity and it never happens because it's just too much trouble.

Now if you are one of those people who are always up for a party and make things happen, God Bless you, please tell me your secret.

For the rest of us, let's set aside some time to specifically make plans and put them on the calendar. Contact those friends you haven't seen, scan the magazines or perform a Google search for whatever it is you want to do and then schedule it. Just Go, It'll Be Fun!

Life is so much more interesting when we have things to look forward to today or in the future.

"Everything you want is outside your comfort zone."

- Robert Allen

Write it Down!

Identify ten things that you and/or
your family can do and then schedule
them on your calendar.

Twenty| Creating Our Own Stress – Let's Decide what's Important

While driving home from running errands there was this knot in my stomach and a feeling of pressure on my mind. There were so many things I "needed" to get done! Ugh, there just isn't enough time in the day! As my mind raced through the list, not sure if it was divine intervention or what, it suddenly hit me that there were numerous things that I did not *have* to do. Why am I creating all this stress for myself?

Do you ever feel this way? We create all these tasks that weigh on our minds. Maybe it's ironing the pillow cases (okay that's just me. Yes, I let that one go), making character cookies for your child's class instead of stopping by Publix, ordering and sending customized birthday cards when you could just click on Evite, getting those last two bales of pine straw to make the flower beds look just right—when you are the only one who will notice—reading all those junk emails that are sitting in your inbox when you should just delete them, or whatever it is that you expend energy on thinking it needs to be done.

77

In Stephen Covey's book *First Things First*, he talks about the subject of managing our time effectively by organizing all the "stuff" into different categories: Important, Not Important, Urgent, and Not Urgent.[1]

This is an excellent tool/idea to help us get things into perspective. If we eliminate most of the things that fall in the Not Important, Not Urgent categories, it really helps us to focus on the important and urgent items and then *decide* to forego the other entries. It's easier said than done, but it's worth a shot. For me, it's something to get me back to putting my head on straight.

Let's all challenge ourselves to purge those items in the fourth quadrant and like my friend, Dominic from up north says, "forgeta bout it!"

What if we all got clear about where we should spend our time, there would probably be a lot less stress in our lives...well, maybe.

---

[1] Stephen Covey, First Things First (New York: Free Press, 1996).

"The only difference between a rich person and poor person is how they use their time."

- Robert Kiyosaki

Right now take at least 20% of your "to do" list and eliminate it and then don't think about those items again...they're not important!

Twenty-One| Mind Food

We had been visiting family who enjoy having the news on as "background" noise. As the stories of murders, rapes, robberies, conflicts, and all the normal ugliness played, I tried my best to tune it out.

When we returned home, it was back to the regular rituals; one of them is walking our dog Bella. As I strolled down the street with her, a van headed toward us. I watched with trepidation and as it slowed down two men jumped out grabbed me and dragged me into the side door. My dog tried to defend me but they kicked her and then off we went. My heart was beating and I began to sweat! Then suddenly Bella yanked my arm trying to chase a squirrel and I snapped out of the trance-like state of envisioning this awful event.

Has this ever happened to you? Maybe you watch a reality show about significant others cheating and you start looking at your partner with suspicion, or you watch a show about revenge and hatred only to find yourself starting to think like those characters without even realizing it. Or the lyrics of songs convey disrespect towards a certain gender or race and even though consciously you don't think that

81

way, somehow those messages seep into your subconscious mind.

I like to say "feed your body healthy food and you'll have a healthy body," the same goes for "feed your mind healthy messages and you'll have a healthy mind."

Take one week and pay attention to your thoughts; it is amazing what goes on inside our heads. You may have some moments that shock you, I sure have, but unless we pay attention it is easy to just continue on aimlessly. If you aren't comfortable with what is going on inside that noggin then take a look at what you are feeding it and make some changes. Try listening to a different kind of music, turn off the news and if you must watch television, choose programming that only feeds the spirit, read motivational, educational or inspirational material...you know what to do.

All of us have choices about what we can do to be purposeful and create the lives we love and want. Feeding our minds that "healthy food" is one place to start. What do you think?

"The happiness of your life depends upon the quality of your thoughts...take care that you entertain no notions unsuitable to virtue and reasonable nature."

- Marcus Aurelius

Turn off the TV for seven days, play games with the family, talk, read, have fun! Do a mind/spirit detox.

Twenty-Two | Avoiding Permanent Damage

One day I snapped at my husband for coming into my office and standing there. Aggravation and frustration still fresh in my mind from the conference call I had just had with my boss who was rattling off fifty million things, (well it seemed like that many), that my team members and I need to accomplish NOW! Completing all of these tasks NOW was unachievable and the more I thought about it, the shorter my fuse. There I was taking it out on my sweet husband who just wants to tell me something.

Does this ever happen to you? Maybe there is pressure at work, a project you are trying to complete but are constantly interrupted, you're attempting to repair or install something but keep running into challenges or another person said or did something to set you off. Then you find yourself taking it out on your children, spouse, or someone else who has done nothing wrong.

How do we stop the madness? For me, when I realized I was taking my anger out on my hubby, first I felt guilty and then gave him a hug and kiss and said, "I'm sorry for being so cranky," and filled him in on my conference call. Hopefully, that was enough. The next thing I decided to do before I projected this attitude onto anyone else was take a "time out" away from other living beings and write my thoughts and feelings down on paper to get them out of my head.

Here are some other ideas to get what's "eatin us" off our minds:
- take a walk,
- call a friend and vent,
- read,
- watch your favorite show, or
- participate in anything that will change your thoughts to the better.

So the next time someone or something pushes your buttons and you feel that surge of ugliness coming on, take the steps to keep from hurting others and having regret. *You can always say you're sorry but you can never take back hurtful words or actions.*

We all deserve kindness and love. Each of us "own" everything we say and do, so let's avoid causing permanent damage to our relationships and exercise self-control in managing our state of mind. What if we all had that kind of discipline? The therapists out there would probably have a lot more time on their hands.

"Treasure the love you receive above all. It will survive long after you good health has vanished."

- Og Mandino

Write it Down!

Write down the most hurtful things you've done to a friend or loved one and genuinely say you're sorry. The next time you're having a bad day or are cranky remove yourself from others and be sure to tell them they did nothing wrong.

Twenty-Three| How Do We See Ourselves?

We were at a family gathering and a discussion started about health and fitness. I was not enthused to participate, because my workout routine had been quite lax lately and the feeling of being bloated was prevalent. As I was mindlessly reaching for an Oreo, my bother-in-law made a comment that caused me to have a complete paradigm shift. He said "Christine's in good shape"...What? First, he got some major family points for that comment, but what struck me was that suddenly I thought to myself, *a person in "good shape" wouldn't eat this Oreo*. So I then grabbed a banana and decided to go for a run...interesting.

Has this ever happened to you where you have a certain perception of yourself then someone makes a comment or you change your actions then rethink everything? Maybe you've gotten into a workout routine and see yourself as a healthy person, then make healthy choices, or the other side of the coin where you are feeling not so slim and decide, *who cares, just eat that bowl of ice cream, it doesn't matter*. Maybe there's some other vice like drinking or smoking; even though we don't like who we are when over indulging, we beat ourselves up thinking we're not good enough to either stop or implement moderation.

Whatever it is that we want to be, it all starts with seeing ourselves as that person. As always, it all comes back to the conversations we have in our heads. If there is "someone" you want to be start telling yourself that's who you are. Sometimes the toughest "sell" is to ourselves.

It may sound a little cheesy, but for the next three weeks, if you don't already know, think about what qualities you want to possess or how you want to be seen and write it down, speak it, see yourself that way; like they say, "fake it till you make it." It works, but it's a matter of keeping at it until it is second nature and we truly feel it. Our insecurities can sometimes dominate, but it's up to us to persevere.

What if we all could execute and be that person we want to be, what a wonderful, fulfilling life that would be.

"Know your value. Confidence breeds success. Act like the person you want to become, and people will start seeing you as that person."

- Michael Masterson

Write it Down!

Journal all the positive qualities you hold right now as well as those you want to possess. Make copies and have them mounted everywhere, see yourself as that person.

Twenty-Four | Kindness to Ourselves

I was at the gym with the rest of America trying to work off the holiday pounds that have accumulated. While I was panting trying to keep up, I couldn't help but look at the instructor and think, *Gosh, if only I had her arms. While I'm at it, how can I get those abs, and jeez is there any way I can somehow sculpt my legs to look like that?* But then I snapped back to reality and said to myself she's 5'10", blonde, and lean and I'm 5'3" brunette, and stocky. It was then that I gave myself a slap upside the head and told myself, *Stop comparing to someone that you'll never be like.*

Does this ever happen to you? We all look at others at some time or another and compare something. For example we may think, *if only I could be skinny like her; have her skin; have as clean a house; volunteer at school more; have children as well behaved*, whatever it is that we judge against. But then we find out the skinny person has an eating disorder, the beautiful skin is because she spends a fortune on skin care products and goes to the dermatologist regularly, has a cleaning service every week, or the children turn out to be little hellions at home.

Whatever others have or don't have really doesn't matter, because at the end of the day we should only compare ourselves to ourselves. All of us have our strengths and weaknesses. At the end of the day, none of us are any better than the others. All we can do is to keep moving forward and focus on how to improve each day in whatever area that we think there are deficiencies.

When the little angel and the little devil are on your shoulders and you're looking at someone else starting to compare, listen to the angel saying, "Focus on you, don't worry about what someone else looks like or what they have. You're great in your way and no one else can compare."

Kindness—if we are kind not only to others but to ourselves, just think how much more confident and ultimately happier we would be having that mentality.

"It's not what you are that holds you back; it's what you think you're not."

- Denis Waitley

Write it Down!

Write out all the great things about yourself.

About the Author

Christine Roberts is a certified child advocate, a corporate manager of a technology and office products finance firm, a wife, and a mother of two children.

Success in Christine's professional career has come through hard work, diligence and her self-mantra, "Go for it!" Despite facing financial and educational challenges, Christine graduated from Georgia State University's Executive MBA program in May 2002—while working full-time—and rose to the top ranks in every company she has served. She also prioritizes her family by compartmentalizing her work, volunteer, and home life so she can be dedicated in each role she fulfills.

Some of her current community activities include:

- Writer/Columnist: "Motivational Corner" published in *My Forsyth* magazine

- Mentor: Mentor Me North Georgia (formerly Big Brothers, Big Sisters)
- Volunteer – Browns Bridge Church (Northpoint Ministries)
- Compassion International – International child sponsor
- Certified Child Advocate – Advocacy Center in Atlanta, Georgia

Christine is dedicated to encouraging and inspiring others to also "Go for it." Her enthusiasm and ability to inspire others make her a highly regarded and sought-after motivational speaker.

Christine enjoys spending time with her family in the suburbs of Atlanta, Georgia. This is her first book.

Find out more about Christine:

www.ChristineMRoberts.com
&
www.inspirationalmindfood.com